SPECIAL TIMES

A journey through life in
Judaism

Jane A. C. West
Consultant: Laurie Rosenberg

Contents

Published by A & C Black Publishers Limited
36 Soho Square
London W1D 3QY
www.acblack.com

ISBN 978–1–4081–0435–4

Copyright © A & C Black Publishers Limited 2009

Series concept: Suma Din
Series consultant: Lynne Broadbent
Created by Bookwork Ltd, Stroud, UK

A CIP catalogue record for this book is available from the British Library.

A & C Black uses paper produced with elemental chlorine-free pulp, harvested from managed sustainable forests. It is natural, renewable and recyclable. The logging and manufacturing process conform to the environmental regulations of the country of origin.

Printed in China by Leo Paper Products

14 A Jewish boy at his Bar Mitzvah

16 A bride and groom celebrate their marriage

22 The Seder plate of food

How to use this book

People who follow the religion of Judaism are known as **Jews**. This book tells you what it is like to be a Jew and about the special times, customs and beliefs of Jews.

Finding your way

The pages in this book have been carefully planned to make it easy for you to find out about Judaism. Here are two examples with explanations about the different features. Look at the Contents pages too, to read about each section.

Labels tell you what is in a picture.

---

16 **Marriage**

Celebrating a Jewish wedding

Marriage is an important stage in the journey of life. Most Jews believe that it is natural for adults to be married and that it is a partnership for life.

A ketubah

The wedding service

Jewish couples do not eat just before their wedding ceremony. This shows that they are starting their life together with a clean slate.

The marriage takes place under a chuppah, which is a decorated canopy held up by four poles. It symbolises the home that the couple will share together. In the UK, part of the service is in English and part is in Hebrew.

The couple sign the ketubah (the marriage contract). They make their marriage vows to each other and the groom gives his bride a ring.

A chuppah

Elan is 23 and lives in London. He talks about his wedding day.

When I met my wife Ariella, I knew that we were bashert – destined to be soulmates. During the wedding ceremony, I put the veil over her face and promised to look after her and clothe her. She looked so beautiful. After the wedding, we had a traditional **kosher** meal and a huge party with all our friends and family. Everyone wished us mazel tov (good luck).

Case studies give a Jewish person's own experience of a custom described in the section.

Comments give additional information about something specific in a picture.

The bride is wearing a traditional white dress with a veil.

bride and groom are a glass of wine gether, just as they ill in their home on abbat and festivals the future.

he end of the ceremony

person in the synagogue called the chazan sings a ayer and the Rabbi says the seven blessings called the eva B'rachot. At the end of the ceremony, the groom amps on a glass. This symbolises the destruction of the **mple of Solomon** in Jerusalem over 2,500 years go and again in 70 CE. It reminds Jews of their long story and their place in the Jewish community. It also minds them that even in a time of happiness there are nes of sorrow. Everyone wishes the couple mazel tov.

Behold you are consecrated to me with this ring, according to the laws of Moses and Israel.

Over to you...

● Lots of faiths celebrate weddings with food and a party. Does anything else about a Jewish wedding remind you of a wedding you have been to?

A groom breaks a glass. This reminds everyone that sadne exists in the world, together with happiness.

Over to you... asks the reader to think more about their own customs and beliefs and how they compare to Jewish beliefs.

Boxed text gives extra information about a subject on the page.

The importance of names

ewish people believe that names are very important. They hope that the new baby's name will reflect the type of person that the baby will grow up to be.

Meanings

A boy might be given the name Barak, which means 'lightning'. A girl might be called Sarah, which means 'ruler'. Some Jewish people name a baby after a relative who has died. They believe this creates a special link between the baby and its ancestor. Some Jews don't name their baby after living relatives because they think it is bad luck.

Jewish names

Some Jewish people give their children two names. There is an everyday name to use at school and at work and a special **Hebrew** (the Jewish language) name to use in religious ceremonies.

Jews from the Middle East an area of southwest Asia and north Africa) may name a baby after a living relative.

Over to you...

● Does your name have a meaning? Why was it chosen for you?

● Does anyone else in your family have the same name as you?

● Do you have more than one name?

Prayer of thanksgiving

The mother of the baby says a prayer of thanksgiving for her baby. This prayer is for a baby daughter:

"May it be Your will, my God and God of the foremothers, to guard the life of this girl from sickness and accident and sustain her. Heal me, her mother, and give me strength for her sake. Since this girl trusts in me to nurture and protect her, I must trust in You to nurture and protect me."

Jews whose families were from eastern Europe often name their babies after a dead relative.

Quotes come from Jewish teachings.

Bold words in the text are explained more fully in the glossary on page 30.

Captions give a short description of a picture.

Welcoming a new baby

The birth of a child is a time to celebrate. For Jews, it is a time to give thanks to God. They welcome a baby boy and a baby girl in different ways: some traditional, some more unusual.

Welcoming a son

On the eighth day after a baby boy's birth, the family has a Brit Milah ceremony to welcome him into the Jewish **faith**. A highly trained and educated man called a mohel very carefully removes the baby's foreskin covering the penis. This is called circumcision.

The Brit Milah is a symbol that remembers and celebrates a **covenant** (agreement) between God and the Jewish people. God promised to look after the people, and Abraham, the founder of Judaism, promised that the people would obey God.

A little girl welcomes her new baby sister.

A new baby joins the family, which is an important part of Jewish life.

Welcoming a daughter

The celebration for the birth of a baby girl is called the Simchat Bat. There is no set celebration, so people have created their own traditions. Some parents name their baby at the **synagogue** (Jewish place of worship). They do this on the day of rest, called the **Shabbat** (also the Sabbath), and share a meal afterwards. Others invite family and friends to a party on a different day to share in the joy. Some say prayers, with a special blessing over wine, and share a festive meal.

A lifelong commitment

The naming ceremony, either of a girl or a boy, is all about making a lifelong commitment to a Jewish way of life, which is centred around the family and the community. Commitment to Judaism and a Jewish way of life is only possible through the home, which is the core of everything.

Aaron is 7 years old. His family has recently celebrated the birth of his baby sister.

Mum and Dad called my sister Rachel, which is a name from the Bible. They invited their friends and the rest of the family to our home to welcome her. The **Rabbi** (Jewish religious teacher) came too. I gave her a tzedakah (charity) box. This is a tradition in Jewish families. She can collect coins in it and later give them to a charity. The Rabbi said a blessing and then we had a meal, including my favourite: smoked salmon and bagels.

The importance of names

Jewish people believe that names are very important. They hope that the new baby's name will reflect the type of person that the baby will grow up to be.

Meanings

A boy might be given the name Barak, which means 'lightning'. A girl might be called Sarah, which means 'ruler'. Some Jewish people name a baby after a relative who has died. They believe this creates a special link between the baby and its ancestor. Some Jews don't name their babies after living relatives because they think it is bad luck.

Jewish names

Some Jewish people give their children two names. There is an everyday name to use at school and at work and a special **Hebrew** (the Jewish language) name to use in religious ceremonies.

Jews from the Middle East (an area of southwest Asia and north Africa) may name a baby after a living relative.

Over to you...

● Does your name have a meaning? Why was it chosen for you?

● Does anyone else in your family have the same name as you?

● Do you have more than one name?

Prayer of thanksgiving

The mother of the baby says a prayer of thanksgiving for her baby. This prayer is for a baby daughter:

"May it be Your will, my God and God of the foremothers, to guard the life of this girl from sickness and accident and sustain her. Heal me, her mother, and give me strength for her sake. Since this girl trusts in me to nurture and protect her, I must trust in You to nurture and protect me."

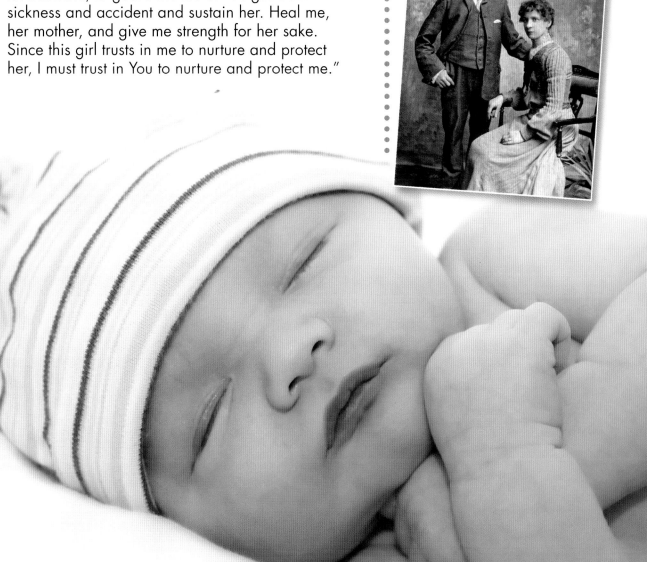

Jews whose families were from eastern Europe often name their babies after a dead relative.

Learning about the Jewish faith

Jews believe that education is very important in order to keep the Jewish faith alive. They believe that learning is something that people should do all their lives.

Learning at school

Jewish children learn about their faith at school, at home and in their synagogue. In the UK, some children go to Jewish schools, which teach Jewish traditions and culture as well as the subjects taught at every other school. Other children go to ordinary schools, but also attend classes in their local synagogue. They learn about Judaism and Hebrew, the language of Jewish prayer.

The Shema

The Shema is one of the first prayers that Jewish children learn. It reminds Jews that:

- *There is only one God*
- *God is loving and they should love God*
- *God's rules should be obeyed*
- *Parents have a lifelong responsibility to their children*
- *Education and learning is everyone's responsibility*

These Jewish boys are at school in Tunisia. They are reading Hebrew, which is written from right to left.

Jews from different countries have different traditions. This man is wearing a fur hat called a streimel hat.

Studying at shul

The synagogue is the community centre and Jewish place of worship. It is also where many Jews learn about their faith. A synagogue is sometimes called a shul, which means 'school'.

Children from the age of five are taught by a Rabbi or member of the community. This usually happens one afternoon a week or on a Sunday morning. They learn to read, write and speak in Hebrew and study the Jewish Bible, called the **Torah**.

Knowing about Jewish history is important, so children learn about how Moses led the Jews out of slavery in Egypt over 3,000 years ago. They also learn about the Holocaust (the murder of Jews in the Second World War) and about how the state of **Israel** came to be.

A scribe creating a Torah scroll with Jewish children.

Over to you...

● Who teaches you about important things, such as how you should treat other people?

Worshipping at the synagogue

A synagogue is the Jewish place of worship – a house of God. It is also a community centre. It is a friendly place and is like a second home. Children are always welcome there.

Inside the synagogue

In the synagogue, men cover their hair with a cap called a kippah. It reminds them that God is above them and greater than them. It can also show which football team they support! Sometimes married women wear a hat or a headscarf.

The Torah (the Jewish holy book) is written on a scroll or set of scrolls. These are kept in a special cupboard in the synagogue, covered by a beautifully embroidered curtain. The cupboard is called the **Ark**. Above the Ark burns the Eternal Lamp. God told Moses to keep a lamp always burning.

A Rabbi removes one of the scrolls from the Ark. Today, in progressive communities, both women and men can be Rabbis.

These boys are all wearing a kippah as a sign of respect.

School boys singing in a Jewish choir in London. Many Jewish prayers are sung.

The service in a synagogue

People sometimes talk during the **service** in a synagogue, but they don't talk when the Ark is opened or when prayers are being sung. Singing is very important because Jews believe that God gave people their voices.

In the UK, the service is mostly in Hebrew with some English. Services are given in Hebrew all over the world, so Jews can go to a synagogue anywhere in the world and have no language problem. They will feel welcome wherever there is a synagogue.

Jewish holy book

The Torah is the name for the first five books of the Hebrew Bible. It offers guidance to Jewish people on how to live and behave. The word 'torah' means 'to teach'. The Torah contains 613 **mitzvot** *(laws). These include the* **Ten Commandments**, *which God gave to Moses.*

Celebrating coming of age

J ewish boys and girls have special coming of age ceremonies. These show that they are growing up. It also means that they are ready to take an active part in their Jewish community.

This boy is using a yad (silver pointer) to help him to read the Torah. It's not easy because there are no vowels, just consonants, and no notes.

Celebrating Bat and Bar Mitzvah

Girls come of age and become Bat Mitzvah when they are 12 years old. Boys become Bar Mitzvah when they are 13 years old.

The ceremony takes place at the synagogue where the children read from the Torah in front of their friends and family. This makes them part of a tradition that goes back 4,000 years. Afterwards, they have a meal at home with their family, or a big party the next day.

Being a member of the community

When Jewish children become Bat or Bar Mitzvah, they take on more adult responsibilities and must follow God's commandments (holy laws). It becomes their responsibility to learn about the Jewish faith, history and traditions. They must learn and follow the Torah's laws and must also keep the law of the country. This is how they can be a good member of the community and a responsible citizen.

Aramaic language

'Bar' meaning 'son', 'bat' meaning 'daughter' and 'mitzvah' meaning 'commandment' are all words in an ancient language called Aramaic. Jesus was born a Jew about 2,000 years ago and this is the language he spoke.

Some Jews wear black clothes that don't attract attention, to show that what they do is more important than what they wear.

Over to you...

● Can you think of any special responsibilities that people take on at different ages?

● Was there, or will there be, a special event for you at a certain age?

Jewish people congratulate a Bar Mitzvah boy.

These boys are praying at the Western Wall. They will remember this special day for the rest of their lives.

Visiting the Western Wall

Some Jewish parents take their son or daughter to the **Kottel** (the Western Wall) in Jerusalem once they become Bar or Bat Mitzvah. It is a very holy and spiritual place for Jewish people, so they come from all over the world to pray in front of it. People write prayers on small pieces of paper and put them in cracks in the wall.

Celebrating a Jewish wedding

Marriage is an important stage in the journey of life. Most Jews believe that it is natural for adults to be married and that it is a partnership for life.

A ketubah

A chuppah

The wedding service

Jewish couples do not eat just before their wedding ceremony. This shows that they are starting their life together with a clean slate.

The marriage takes place under a chuppah, which is a decorated canopy held up by four poles. It symbolises the home that the couple will share together. In the UK, part of the service is in English and part is in Hebrew.

The couple sign the ketubah (the marriage contract). They make their marriage vows to each other and the groom gives his bride a ring.

Élan is 23 and lives in London. He talks about his wedding day.

When I met my wife Ariella, I knew that we were bashert — destined to be soulmates. During the wedding ceremony, I put the veil over her face and promised to look after her and clothe her. She looked so beautiful. After the wedding, we had a traditional **kosher** meal and a huge party with all our friends and family. Everyone wished us mazel tov (good luck).

The bride is wearing a traditional white dress with a veil.

A bride and groom share a glass of wine together, just as they will in their home on Shabbat and festivals in the future.

Over to you...

● Lots of faiths celebrate weddings with food and a party. Does anything else about a Jewish wedding remind you of a wedding you have been to?

The end of the ceremony

A person in the synagogue called the chazan sings a prayer and the Rabbi says the seven blessings called the Sheva B'rachot. At the end of the ceremony, the groom stamps on a glass. This symbolises the destruction of the **Temple of Solomon** in Jerusalem over 2,500 years ago and again in 70 CE. It reminds Jews of their long history and their place in the Jewish community. It also reminds them that even in a time of happiness there are times of sorrow. Everyone wishes the couple mazel tov.

Behold you are consecrated to me with this ring, according to the laws of Moses and Israel.

A groom breaks a glass. This reminds everyone that sadness exists in the world, together with happiness.

Jews in their community

Jews believe that everyone should love and respect themselves and their neighbours. They try to follow the Torah commandment, "Love your neighbour as yourself."

Who is your neighbour?

Most Jews believe that God's laws are meant for everyone. For Jews, everyone is their neighbour, however different they may be. There is a commandment that says Jews must never treat someone from another faith any differently.

Caring for others

God promised to care for His people. He blessed Abraham so that he could care for others. God said, "Through you I will bless all the nations." Caring for others is at the heart of the Jewish faith. Many Jewish adults and children help in old people's homes or visit people who are homeless or in hospital. There are laws in the Torah that tell people to care by:

An important part of the Jewish faith is gemillut hasidim, which means 'care for others'.

- Visiting the sick, called bikkur cholim
- Giving people respect and dignity, called kavod
- Caring or having a good heart, called lev tov
- Being righteous or good. A righteous person is known as a tzedek, and tzedakah means 'charity' or 'helping other people'.

> "You shall not bear grudges against the children of your people, but you shall love your neighbour as yourself: I am the Lord."

This little girl's visit brings joy to her granny, who has been unwell.

Over to you...

● Can you think of any times when you've helped a charity? How did it feel?

● How do you think people who are helped by charity feel?

Why Shabbat is so important

This woman has lit two Shabbat candles. Many Jewish people light a candle for each child in the family.

The Jewish day of rest is called Shabbat (Sabbath). It's a time for the family to get together and celebrate God's creation of the universe.

The start of Shabbat

Shabbat begins when the sun goes down on Friday evening and ends when the first stars appear in the sky on Saturday night. All over the world, Jews try to keep Friday night special.

When Shabbat begins, Jews light two candles. These symbolise the commandments to remember and observe Shabbat. People may go to the synagogue on Friday evening. When they come home, parents bless their children. They all drink sweet, red wine, wash their hands in water poured from a cup, then eat challah, a lovely, sweet bread, and have a wonderful, traditional meal.

Benji is 11 and lives in Scotland. He talks about Shabbat.

We are not supposed to work on Shabbat, so on Friday afternoon I come home straight from school and help Mum get things ready. We clean the house and get the food ready before sunset. In winter, Dad tries to get home from work early so that he's there when Mum lights the Shabbat candles. Before our meal, Dad blesses me and my sister. Then he says Kiddush, a prayer remembering why we have Shabbat.

Challah (plural challot) is a sweet, eggy bread. Two challot are used at Shabbat.

Jews eat challah and drink red wine to remind them that God has always provided for them.

A day to enjoy

On Saturday morning, Jewish families go to the synagogue. Some Jews do not use technology or motor vehicles during Shabbat because it is a day of rest, so they walk to the synagogue. Shabbat is a time for prayer and a time to enjoy things, such as good food. After the service, friends and family gather for lunch.

After dark on Saturday is **Havdalah**. It marks the end of Shabbat and is the start of the new week. A special plaited candle with six wicks is lit. It is a time for people to rest and they are not allowed to be creative. They say it is time 'to be a creature, not a creator'.

In six days, the Lord made Heaven and Earth, and on the seventh day he rested and was refreshed.

The importance of food for Jews

Food is an important part of all Jewish celebrations and festivals, even when it is not eaten because it is a time for fasting. Many Jews follow rules about what they can eat, called **Kashrut**.

This shop has a special section selling kosher food for Pesach (also known as Passover).

Kosher food

Kashrut rules in the Torah say what food Jews may eat and how it should be prepared. Food that obeys these rules is called kosher. For example, Jews can eat meat only from certain animals, such as cows, sheep and chickens. They cannot eat pigs, rabbits or birds of prey. The animals must be killed in a way that causes the least distress, because God loves all creatures. Only a trained, very religious man can do this.

Abigail is 9 and lives in New Zealand. She explains one of the Four Questions.

Pesach is my favourite festival because the whole family is there. I'm the youngest so I get to ask the Four Questions. One of the questions is, "Why is it that on other nights we eat leavened bread, but on this night we eat only matzah?" Then Grandpa Eli or Dad says, "When the Jewish slaves left Egypt, they didn't have time to bake their bread. They baked it in the sun, making unleavened matzah."

Matzah is unleavened bread. It is made without yeast so is very flat, like a cracker.

A father breaks the matzah at the beginning of the Seder meal.

The Seder plate helps to tell the story of the Jews' escape from Egypt. Each item of food is a symbol of that journey.

Pesach

Pesach is a festival that remembers when Moses led the Jews out of Egypt from slavery to freedom. The Pesach meal is called **Seder**. It is one of the most important meals that Jewish families have at home, when children learn the Pesach story. In the centre of the table is a plate with food that symbolises the story. One food is flat bread called matzah. Over the eight days of Pesach, only matzah can be eaten, and no bread.

The joyful evening is one of curiosity, prayer, singing and eating. The younger children ask the Four Questions. This is a Jewish tradition and the questions and answers help them to remember their history and what Jews have been through.

Respecting older people

Old age is a significant part of life's journey. The Torah says that growing old is a blessing. The Hebrew word for 'old' is zakein, and it also means 'wise'.

A young Jewish girl with her grandfather. Grandparents are included in all parts of Jewish tradition.

Being a grandparent

The centre of Jewish life is the family, and grandparents play an important part. They can tell stories and share their knowledge and experiences to give their grandchildren a better understanding of Jewish traditions and beliefs. The Torah tells Jews to respect older people because of what they have seen, done and suffered.

> *You shall rise before an aged person and you shall respect the elderly, and you shall fear your God.*

Ruth often asks her zayde (grandfather) for advice.

Jeremy is 65 and lives in Canada. He has just retired.

I have recently retired from work. Some of my friends joked that it was time for me to put on my slippers. That's not for me. The **Talmud** (Jewish holy law) says, "Today is the time to do; tomorrow, to reap the reward." This means God has given me more days – more life – and there are still things he wants me to do – things to achieve. I've been on this Earth a long time and I've still got a lot to give. Here I come!

Over to you...

● Some people never retire – artists and writers, for example. Do you know any older people who are still working?

● Do you know any older people who have done exciting things since they retired?

Enjoying family traditions

On special holidays and religious celebrations, it is traditional for families to gather at the grandparents' home. Meals are filled with the smells, tastes, songs and stories of the Jewish people. Jews think it is important to remember and talk about their traditions, creating memories for the next generation.

In some families, parents and grandparents live far away from each other. Grandparents are getting used to talking or even singing with their grandchildren over the internet!

This man is praying from a siddur (the Jewish prayer book) at a synagogue in north Africa. He is studying in the same way that his Muslim neighbours do.

Death and the afterlife

Jews believe that death is part of God's plan. Life is a gift to be celebrated, but everyone dies one day. This is sad, but natural, and nothing to be scared of.

A Jewish man mourns the death of his father, but he knows that his dad will always live in his heart.

Enjoying life

Jews tend not to focus on death, believing that it is simply the next step in their journey. They believe that life is very precious and that everyone must ensure that they enjoy every moment of their life on Earth.

When people die, their lives are remembered and celebrated by their friends and families. The focus is on remembering the good things that have happened and celebrating the joy of each life.

The afterlife

The afterlife is called Olam Ha-Ba. It means 'The World to Come' and it's a bit like the Christian Heaven. Jews believe that every good person goes there when they die, whatever their beliefs. Jews are waiting for the **Mashiach** to come. Jews believe he is the one, chosen by God, who will put an end to all the evil in the world. They believe that the world will then be perfect and the dead will be brought back to life.

When someone dies, their **soul** returns to be with God.

The dust [the body] returns to the dust as it was, but the spirit returns to God who gave it.

A man comforts his daughter after a loved one has died. Parents explain death and discuss it openly with children.

When a loved one dies

Immediately after a death, the family of the person who has died is helped by the community. The family really has nothing to do. Friends bring food for everybody and look after them.

The mitzvot (laws set down in the Torah) take Jewish people through the period and process of mourning. They tell people all the things they have to do for a year after the death of a loved one. Many people find this helps them to get through what can be a very difficult and lonely time for them.

Over to you...

● What do you believe happens when people die?

● Do you know anyone who believes that there is life after death?

Remembering those we loved

Jewish people perform lots of rituals when someone dies. Many of these are to help the friends and family left behind. Others are to show respect for the dead person.

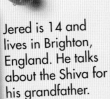

Jered is 14 and lives in Brighton, England. He talks about the Shiva for his grandfather.

During Shiva for Grandpa, loads of people came to visit. We didn't have to worry about food because everything was done for us. We laughed a lot as we remembered Grandpa's jokes. We also looked through photograph albums and talked about his life. It was good to see how much he had done during his life and how much he had achieved. It made me sad to think he was gone. I'll miss him loads, but I know we'll meet again.

Shiva

When a Jewish person dies, their close relatives sit **Shiva** for seven days. Shiva is Hebrew for 'seven'. It is a period of mourning. The closest family sit on low chairs during Shiva to show that they are feeling down and low because of the death.

Every day, a Rabbi visits the family's home and gives an evening service. An adult mourner says a special prayer called the Kaddish. A candle is lit that burns for the seven days of Shiva.

These Jewish headstones are in a graveyard in London. Some words are in English and some are in Hebrew.

Jewish people have left stones on the grave to show their respect.

R. I. P.

OSKAR SCHINDLER
8. 4. 1908 – 9. 10. 1974

DER UNVERGESSLICHE
LEBENRETTER
120 VERFOLGER

The funeral ceremony

Jews arrange a levoyah (a funeral) as quickly as possible after someone has died, usually the day after death. Before the funeral, the body is washed and wrapped in a white sheet. This shows that the rich and poor are equal in the sight of God. The body is never left alone, as a sign of respect.

During the ceremony, prayers are said and the Rabbi gives a blessing. The closest relatives make a small tear in their clothes. This is to show their sadness. They will wear these clothes throughout the week of Shiva.

Then the dead person is buried in a grave. A headstone is put on the grave, usually a year after the funeral, and family and friends bring small pebbles to put on it. This shows that the person is cared for, even after death.

The grave of Oskar Schindler, a Christian who helped Jews during the Second World War.

Jewish people also light a memorial candle at home on the anniversary of someone's death. They leave it to burn for 25 hours.

Blessed are you, Lord our God,
Ruler of the universe, the true Judge.

Glossary and more information

Ark The cupboard in a *synagogue*, in which the *Torah* scrolls are kept.

covenant An agreement. In the Bible, God made many covenants with the Jewish people.

faith A system of religious belief.

Havdalah A ceremony that marks the end of *Shabbat*.

Hebrew The ancient language in which the Jewish Bible and Jewish prayers are writtten. Also, a living language spoken in *Israel*.

Israel The Jewish homeland. A small country in the Middle East.

Jew One who follows the religion of Judaism. Also, someone descended from the first Jewish people of ancient times.

Kashrut The laws that tell *Jews* what foods they can eat, and how the food should be prepared and eaten.

kosher Food that is ok for Jewish people to eat, according to *Kashrut* laws.

Kottel A Jewish holy place in Jerusalem. The remains of a wall built in 515 BCE that once enclosed the Second *Temple of Solomon*.

Mashiach A leader chosen by God, for whom Jews are waiting. Jews believe this person will help remove evil from the world.

mitzvot A set of holy laws, commandments and instructions for Jewish people.

Pesach The celebration to remember the freeing of Jews from slavery in Egypt.

Rabbi A Jewish religious teacher, often the head of a Jewish community.

Seder A special meal that families have at home to celebrate *Pesach*.

service A ceremony when people meet to pray and worship together.

Shabbat The Jewish day of rest, from sunset on Friday to nightfall on Saturday.

Shiva The period of seven days that Jews spend in mourning, after the burial of a close relative.

soul The spiritual part of a person, including the mind, separate from the body.

synagogue A Jewish place of worship.

Talmud An encyclopedia of Jewish law taken from the *Torah*, with explanations to help people to follow the laws.

Temple of Solomon The temple built by King Solomon of *Israel*, as instructed by God. It was destroyed, rebuilt and destroyed again.

Ten Commandments The ten laws given by God to Moses, which told the people how they should live.

Torah The first five books of the Hebrew Bible, which are the same as those in the Old Testament.

Things to do

Find out about the different forms of Judaism. These include Orthodox Judaism, Reform Judaism and Liberal Judaism.

Ask your teacher to help you to arrange a visit to a synagogue near you. You can find your nearest synagogue on this website: www.somethingjewish. co.uk/uk_synagogues/index.htm. Or you can contact the Board of Deputies of British Jews to ask for information about your nearest synagogue. Visit its website: www.bod.org.uk

Visit a Jewish graveyard. Treat it with respect. Find out why many headstones carry this symbol ✡. It is called the Star of David and is very important to Jews.

The Jewish New Year is called Rosh Hashanah. It happens in September. Find out more about this special time.

More information

Find out more about Judaism on these websites.

Websites

www.bbc.co.uk/religion/religions/judaism
This BBC website has lots of information about Judaism, including the history, customs and holy days and different forms of Judaism.

www.akhlah.com
There is masses of information on this website of the Jewish Children's Learning Network. You can find out about people and stories in the Torah as well as Jewish traditions, holidays and heroes. There is also a section on learning Hebrew.

www.chabad.org
This useful website for children has information about Orthodox Judaism. The kids section includes games, ideas for activities, recipes, stories, songs and videos.

www.reformjudaism.org.uk
Find out lots about Reform Judaism on this website. You can look for your nearest synagogue, and there is an A–Z section with information about Jewish beliefs and customs.

www.holidays.net/highholydays
Learn about the important Jewish holy days of Rosh Hashanah (New Year) and Yom Kippur (Day of Atonement). Type 'passover' instead of 'highholydays' into the website address to find out about the festival of Pesach (Passover).

www.reonline.org.uk
This website has separate sections for teachers and children. It has links to other useful websites where you can find out about Judaism and other religions.

Index

Picture credits

The publisher would like to thank the following for their kind permission to reproduce their photographs

Position key: c=centre; b=bottom; t=top; l=left; r=right

1c: iStockphoto; 2cr: Tony Kurdzuk/Star Ledger/Corbis; 2tr: Paul Gapper/World Religions Photo Library; 2br: Paul Gapper/ World Religions Photo Library; 4bc: Yuri Arcurs/iStockphoto; 6bl: Sean Warren/iStockphoto; 7tc: iStockphoto; 7cr: Noam Armonn/Shutterstock; 8cl: Rohit Seth/Shutterstock; 9cr: Duncan Walker/iStockphoto; 9bc: Elaine Hudson/ Shutterstock; 10cl: Paul Gapper/World Religions Photo Library; 11tc: R Schogger/World Religions Photo Library; 12bl: Christine Osborne/World Religions Photo Library; 13tc: Paul Gapper/World Religions Photo Library; 14cl: Nancy Louie/iStockphoto; 15bc: Bob Munro/World Religions Photo Library; 15tc: Paul Gapper/World Religions Photo Library; 16c: Joy Powers/iStockphoto; 16bl: Yuri Arcurs/Shutterstock; 17tc: Tony Kurdzuk/Star Ledger/Corbis; 17br: Erez Ben Simon/World Religions Photo Library; 18cl: Mikhail Lavrenov/iStockphoto; 19tc: Monkey Business Images/Shutterstock; 20cl: Howard Sandler/Shutterstock; 20bl: Lisa F Young/Shutterstock; 21cr: Pavelr/Shutterstock; 21tc: Christine Osborne/World Religions Photo Library; 22c: Monkey Business Images/Shutterstock; 22cl: Christine Osborne/World Religions Photo Library; 23c: iStockphoto; 23tc: Noam Armonn/Shutterstock; 24bc: Lisa F Young/Shutterstock; 25tl: Carme Balcells/Shutterstock; 25c: Christine Osborne/World Religions Photo Library; 26cl: Mike Cherim/iStockphoto; 27tc: Sheryl Griffin/iStockphoto; 28cl: Lisa F Young/Shutterstock; 28br: Christine Osborne/World Religions Photo Library; 29tc: Bob Munro/World Religions Photo Library; 29br: R Schogger/World Religions Photo Library

Cover photograph: © Paul Doyle/Alamy